CLOSER LOOK AT

TIDAL WAVES AND FLOODING

Michael Flaherty

COPPER BEECH BOOKS
Brookfield, Connecticut

© Aladdin Books Ltd 1996
Designed and produced by
Aladdin Books Ltd
28 Percy Street
London W1P 0LD

*First published in the United States
in 1998 by*
Copper Beech Books,
an imprint of
The Millbrook Press
2 Old New Milford Road
Brookfield, Connecticut 06804

Editor
Alex Edmonds

Designer
Gary Edgar-Hyde

Picture Research
Brooks Krikler Research

Front cover illustration
Gary Edgar-Hyde

Illustrator
Mike Saunders

Printed in Belgium
5 4 3 2 1

Library of Congress Cataloging-in-Publication Data
Flaherty, Michael.
Tidal waves and flooding / Michael Flaherty ;
illustrated by Mike Saunders.
p. cm. — (Closer look at)
Includes index.
Summary: Explains the causes and effects of tidal waves and
flooding and examines their environmental impact.
ISBN 0-7613-0866-0 (lib. bdg.)
1. Tsunamis—Environmental aspects—Juvenile literature.
2. Floods—Environmental aspects—Juvenile literature.
[1. Tsunamis. 2. Floods.] I. Sanders, Mike, ill.
II. Title. III. Series: Closer look at (Brookfield, Conn.)
GC221.2.F54 1998   98-18130
551.47'024—dc21   CIP AC

CONTENTS

INTRODUCTION

Flooding is one of the most destructive natural disasters. It can be caused by many different factors and it can happen almost anywhere in the world. These factors can stem from natural causes, like tidal waves and extreme seasonal weather conditions. Accidents or human activity may also produce them. At its worst, flooding can cause the deaths of thousands of people; at its best, natural seasonal flooding can irrigate and make farming possible where it would otherwise be impossible.

The way that water moves around the earth is called the water cycle. It is estimated that 326 million cubic miles of water are involved in the water cycle. Variations in weather conditions across the globe cause an uneven distribution of all this water. This can lead to extreme drought in some areas while others experience devastating floods.

THE WATER

Water vapor
About 10 million billion gallons of water evaporate into the atmosphere every year. The oceans contribute about 86% of this. Rivers and lakes contribute a further 12%. Vegetation only supplies about 2%. Water vapor (above) is given off by plants usually through their leaves, in a process called transpiration.

HOW IT WORKS

When air rises in the atmosphere, it cools and the water vapor in the air condenses (turns into tiny drops of water). Where the vapor cools, the water becomes visible as clouds, and may return to the earth's surface as rain or snow. Most of this falls into the oceans and other bodies of water. If it falls onto the land it sinks into the earth and may be held as ground water – possibly for thousands of years. But eventually it will seep back into seas, rivers, and lakes, and starts on its way around the water cycle again.

Clouds are made up of millions of tiny droplets of water or ice. Each droplet is smaller than one grain of flour.

From outer space our planet looks like a blue globe. This is because about three quarters of the earth's surface is covered in water. The Pacific, Atlantic, and Indian oceans hold 98% of this water. Glacier ice (right) covers 10% of the earth's land surface.

CYCLE

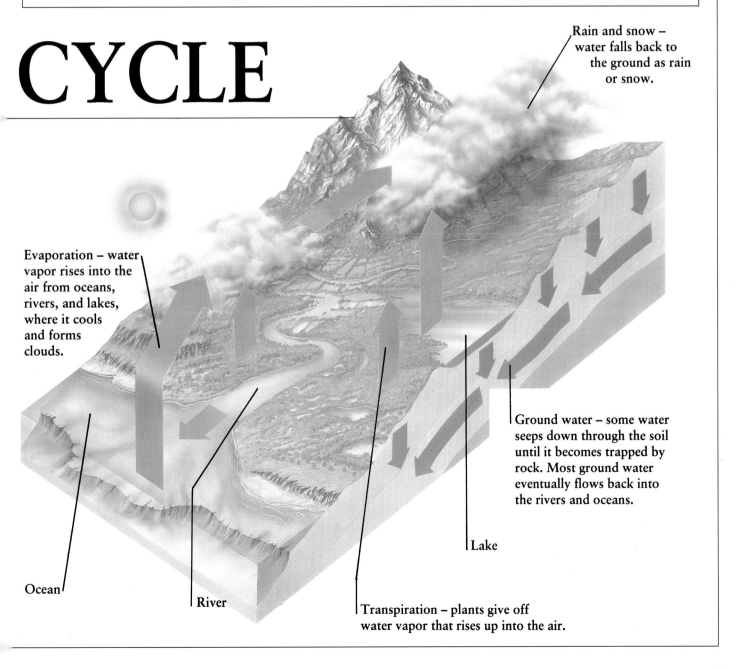

Rain and snow – water falls back to the ground as rain or snow.

Evaporation – water vapor rises into the air from oceans, rivers, and lakes, where it cools and forms clouds.

Ground water – some water seeps down through the soil until it becomes trapped by rock. Most ground water eventually flows back into the rivers and oceans.

Lake

Ocean

River

Transpiration – plants give off water vapor that rises up into the air.

Wild waves

Many coastlines suffer from serious flooding due to unusually high tides. When spring tides (see page 9) come into contact with particularly stormy weather (below) they can cause flooding. The damage caused to shorelines, housing, boats, and ships is often serious.

The waters of the oceans and some large lakes are affected by the wind, moon, and sun. Winds cause great volumes of water to travel around the planet in the form of ocean currents. They travel at 1–5 knots, and move in big, circular paths. The water of the oceans is constantly moving, and as it washes along coastlines it affects the climate.

SEAS IN

WAVE MOVEMENT

Waves on the sea are like ripples on a pond. The force of the wind moving along the surface of the sea causes the particles of water to move up and down in a circular motion, ending in the same place that they started. This circular motion may cause the wave to break, or turn over, at its peak, as can be seen at the shore. Only then does the wave make the water move along.

The gravitational pull of the moon (right) on the oceans is greater than that of the sun. Ocean waters on the side of the earth facing the moon are pulled the most, giving a high tide. There is also a less noticeable high tide on the other side of the earth.

MOTION

Spring and neap tides

The moon and the sun have an effect on the oceans, called tides. Tides are the daily rise and fall of sea level. High and low tides occur about six hours apart. The distance in height between high and low tide is called the tidal range. When the earth, moon, and sun are in a line the combined pull of the moon and sun causes the highest and lowest tides. These are called spring tides. When the sun and the moon are at a right angle with the earth, their pulls work against one another. This results in the lowest tidal range and is called the neap tide. Spring and neap tides both happen twice a month.

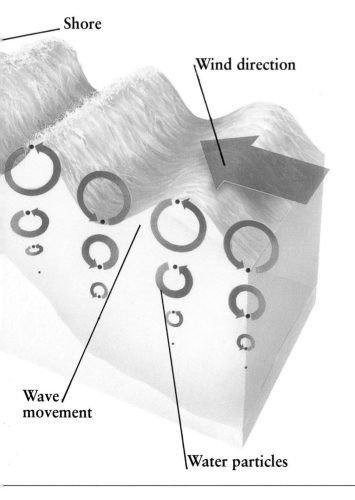

Shore

Wind direction

Wave movement

Water particles

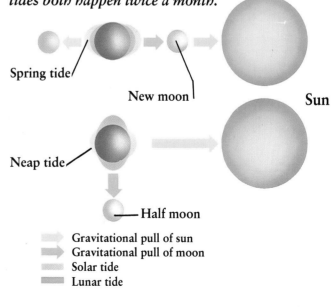

Spring tide

New moon

Sun

Neap tide

Half moon

Gravitational pull of sun
Gravitational pull of moon
Solar tide
Lunar tide

Tropical sea storms can only brew when the sea's surface temperature is at least 78° F. The rising moist, warm air forms storm clouds. Contact with areas of low air pressure then leads to high winds. The earth's rotation makes these winds spin, producing a tropical storm. As this storm crashes into the coast, it brings with it huge waves called storm surges.

WALLS OF

STORM SURGES

Tropical storms cause storm surges. Powerful winds churn the sea into high waves. These may reach the coastline when the center of the storm is about 112 miles off shore. As the storm hits the shore, a mound of water beneath the storm's eye overwhelms the land. Sea levels rise above the height of protective sand dunes on shore. As the sea rushes onto land it floods land behind them.

Dune defenses

ON CLOSER INSPECTION
– *The storm arrives*

When a hurricane, such as Hurricane Gilbert (right), hits land it causes most damage. As the storm smashes into the coast, it brings with it huge waves – storm surges that crash onto the land. Around the center, or eye of the storm, winds can reach 124 mph.

WATER

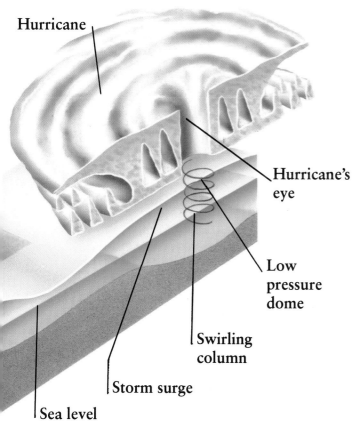

Hurricane

Hurricane's eye

Low pressure dome

Swirling column

Storm surge

Sea level

Five waterspouts seen in the Adriatic Sea in August 1958.

WATERSPOUTS

When rising warm, moist air meets cold, dry air, they form a whirling column. This sucks up water as mist and spray, forming a waterspout, which can rise almost 4 miles above the sea. It may even be strong enough to suck up schools of fish. Waterspouts look spectacular, but do little damage and last an hour at most.

Volcanic waves

Erupting volcanoes or islands formed by volcanic eruptions under the sea (below) may cause tsunamis similar to those caused by earthquakes. The volcanic island of Krakatoa exploded in 1883, producing a tsunami 100 ft high.

Earthquakes under the ocean release a lot of energy in the form of shock waves, also called seismic waves. This burst of energy in the ocean crust makes the seabed jolt and the water above vibrate. The waves formed are often wrongly called tidal waves. The correct name is tsunami.

TSUNAMI!

Transform fault

Oceanic ridge

Subduction zone

Oceanic crust

THE MOVING EARTH

The earth's crust is made up of plates that are constantly moving. Pressure builds up where the plates meet. When the pressure becomes too great the plates jolt into a new position, resulting in an earthquake. This occurs at a transform fault where plates slide past each other and in a subduction zone where plates collide and the edge of one is dragged down into the mantle.

The tsunami smashes down on the coast, sweeping away everything in its path.

ON CLOSER INSPECTION
– Damage control

Earthquake waves cross the ocean in minutes. Seismograph stations (right) detect them and plot the center of the earthquake. Water levels are monitored across the ocean. This allows warnings to be given to places in a tsunami's path.

When an earthquake happens below the ocean floor, part of the seabed may be forced up.

When the tsunami gets closer to the shore, its waves become closer together and taller.

The seismic waves make the sea floor jolt, which creates huge sea waves.

TIDAL WAVE FACTS

Tsunamis or tidal waves can travel at speeds of 500 mph. As they approach the shallower shore, the wave slows down and builds up to a huge height. Waves pile up as faster waves come in from behind. They grow to over 100 ft before breaking over the coast with disastrous consequences. The Great Wave of Kanagawa (below), painted in 1831 by Hokusai of Japan, shows boats being tossed around by a tsunami.

Going up!

The Yellow River, or Huang Ho, and the Mississippi (below) have deposited so much mud and silt over the years that their riverbeds have risen above the surrounding countryside. Sections of the Mississippi's banks have had to be raised by as much as 23 ft since 1882.

Rivers are one of the most important natural forces to shape the land. A river valley is gradually cut away and broadened by water over time, building up a flat floodplain of mud and rock. Periodic flooding spills onto these plains laying down more fertile sediment. Floodplains can prevent further floods by keeping water from overflowing until the river level drops.

THE

AGING BUT DANGEROUS

Rivers have three main stages of life – youth, maturity, and old age. In its old age the river contains the greatest volume of water, although it travels more slowly as it gets older. The Mississippi (left) is a very old river, which is why it floods very frequently.

THE RIVER – A LIFE STORY

The earth is continually being worn away – even the Himalayas will be reduced to low-lying plains one day. Rivers are one of the forces responsible for these changes. They erode land, transport sediment and materials along the river valley, and deposit them farther along and eventually out to sea. These activities have created many of the spectacular landforms of today.

ON CLOSER INSPECTION
– *"China's sorrow"*

The Huang Ho (Yellow River – see right) in China is also called "China's Sorrow." It has claimed more lives than any other natural feature on the planet. The Yellow River has also shifted its course over the centuries in spectacular fashion – by over 600 miles.

RIVER

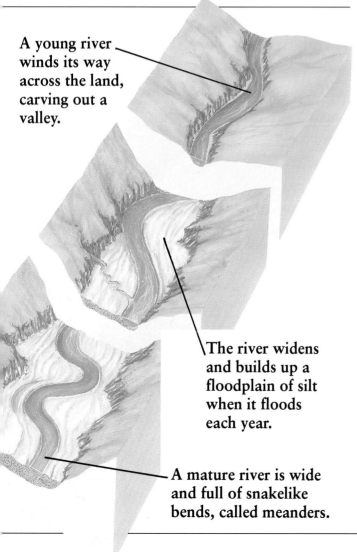

A young river winds its way across the land, carving out a valley.

The river widens and builds up a floodplain of silt when it floods each year.

A mature river is wide and full of snakelike bends, called meanders.

THE NILE

Rivers can be prevented from running their natural course by building dams. The Aswan Dam across the Nile (below) has prevented most of the river's rich sediment from being deposited farther downstream over the last two decades. Instead, the fertile river deposits stay on the bed of Lake Nasser behind the dam, where they do no good. Farmers then have to rely on chemical fertilizers to feed their crops.

Rain, rain, rain
Torrential rain rapidly delivers huge amounts of water to the soil. The water is quickly soaked up by the soil until it can hold no more. At the same time, rivers overflow their banks and flood the surrounding waterlogged land.

Rivers flood for many reasons. In mountainous regions, melting snow and ice may swell and overflow the river in spring. Heavy rainfall, as in the monsoon season in Asia, can also produce more water than rivers can cope with, causing flooding. During spring tides, high winds may cause storm tides that surge up the river and flood the land (see page 8).

RIVER

MISSISSIPPI MADNESS
The Mississippi River system is vast. It covers 31 U.S. states and two Canadian provinces. The area around the lower Mississippi (below) used to be considered one of the most dangerous flood areas in the world. In 1927, the river flooded an area of nearly 17,237,000 acres causing extensive damage to cities and towns.

On Closer Inspection
– *Wadi*

A wadi is a river channel found in mountainous desert regions that only floods in the rainy season. The rest of the time it is dry. But, heavy rains in the mountains can cause flash floods that sweep along these channels, carrying rocks and mud with them.

FLOODING

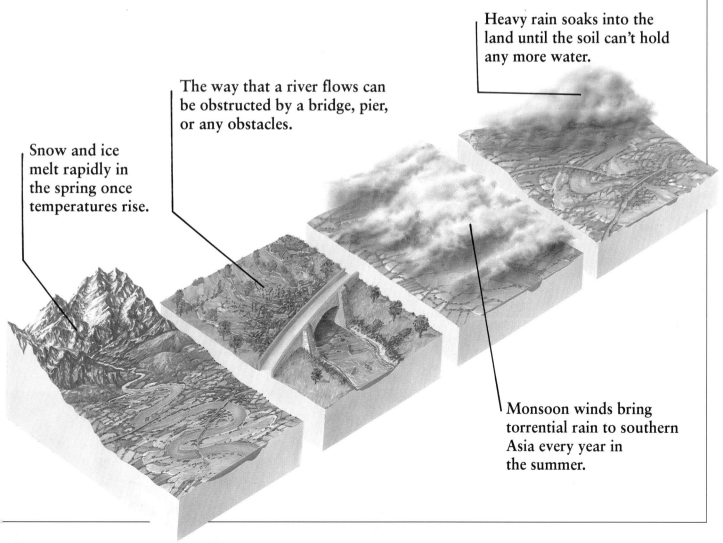

Heavy rain soaks into the land until the soil can't hold any more water.

The way that a river flows can be obstructed by a bridge, pier, or any obstacles.

Snow and ice melt rapidly in the spring once temperatures rise.

Monsoon winds bring torrential rain to southern Asia every year in the summer.

The horror!
Statistics show that river floods kill nearly twice as many people as 18 other types of natural disaster put together. We can see the suffering of flood victims (above).

Flooding is the most widespread of all natural disasters. It causes the most damage, therefore, to life and property. Flooding destroys homes leaving people without shelter. It can kill livestock and plants that people depend upon to live. So famine as well as disease can be a very real danger after a major flood.

DEVASTATION

1987 "HURRICANE"

In the fall of 1987, a freak storm crossed the Atlantic Ocean heading toward Europe (left). Its winds strengthened as it neared the coast of northern France, causing great waves that flooded Normandy farmland, laying waste to crops and killing livestock. The land was rendered useless for five years.

Houses and cars are engulfed in water as flooding from the 1987 "hurricane" threatens a house in England.

ON CLOSER INSPECTION – *Lisbon, 1755*

In 1755, Lisbon was destroyed by a massive earthquake, measuring 8.75 on the Richter scale. It produced a tsunami that crashed over the city killing 60,000 people. Damage caused by the earthquake alone was huge (see right).

MONSOON

Each year, during the summer in India, the monsoon winds bring torrential rain and flooding to many cities and towns. The city of Cherrapunji (below) receives a yearly average of 240 inches per year, one of the highest annual rainfall totals in the world.

A TOWN IN RUINS

Floods break power lines and rupture gas mains, causing fires throughout a flooded city. Telephone lines go down. Highways and railroad tracks are torn apart and bridges are swept away. Fresh water supplies are contaminated, allowing the spread of diseases, such as cholera and typhoid.

Jakarta in Indonesia is built on land near the coast. Its poorer inhabitants are forced to live in badly built homes on the low-lying land. Regular sea floods cause damage time and again to their flimsy houses, leaving them homeless (below).

Through the ages people have always settled near sources of water for drinking, fishing, farming, transportation, and trade. Cities can be threatened by flooding from either the rise in river levels or from the sea. In the developing world, even today, many cities are still built in areas threatened by regular flooding.

CONSTANT

ARNO FLOODS
The city of Florence in Italy sits on the Arno River. Floods have been a threat to the city since A.D. 1117 when they were first recorded. In 1966, heavy rain caused the river to flood. Buildings, frescos, and many works of art were damaged beyond repair by the debris-laden waters.

THREAT

The gates of the barrier sit on the riverbed in the open position. When the water level rises, they are rotated by large, wheellike structures so that they are in a vertical position and close the openings between the piers, sealing off the river.

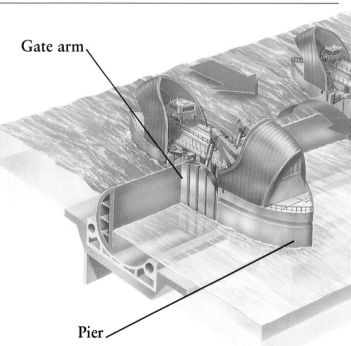

Gate arm

Pier

THAMES RIVER BARRIER

In 1953, the level of the Thames River in London, England was recorded at over three feet higher than its spring-tide level. Many of the river's protective embankments proved too low to hold back floodwater. Many areas in London, including its underground railroad system, are below sea level and therefore at risk from flooding. In 1984, a tidal flood defense system called the Thames River Barrier was opened. Located across the river at Woolwich, it consists of 10 gates that can be closed to protect against future tidal surges.

variety of measures have been devised to reduce the effects of flooding. Modern technology has improved early warning systems, allowing people to evacuate places under threat. Water levels of rivers likely to flood are monitored in combination with weather reports of future heavy rain and snow.

Tree replanting

Around the foothills of the Himalayan mountains (above), a planned scheme for replanting trees will provide firewood for locals, and help to prevent the runoff of heavy rains, and the resulting flooding, by keeping the soil in place.

COUNTER

BANGLADESH PREPARES

In Bangladesh, 63 flood shelters were built to house people safely during seasonal flooding. Built 13 ft above ground, they protected 350,000 people during floods caused by the 1991 cyclone. The more traditional method of using sandbags to prevent floodwaters from spreading is also used (below).

BUILDING DIKES

Dikes and levees (riverbanks) are built (above) to prevent both coastal and river flooding. Much of the Netherlands is below sea level and the country relies on dikes to hold back the sea. Levees built along the Mississippi help control many of its unpredictable floods.

Japan is one country that is particularly prone to tsunamis. A system of coastal defenses has been built, which uses huge concrete slabs linked together, which hold back the floodwaters (right).

MEASURES

WHAT CAN WE DO?

To control river flooding, dams can be built across valleys, with sluice gates to control water flow. Such dams also supply water for irrigation, hydroelectric power, and constant freshwater supplies (right).

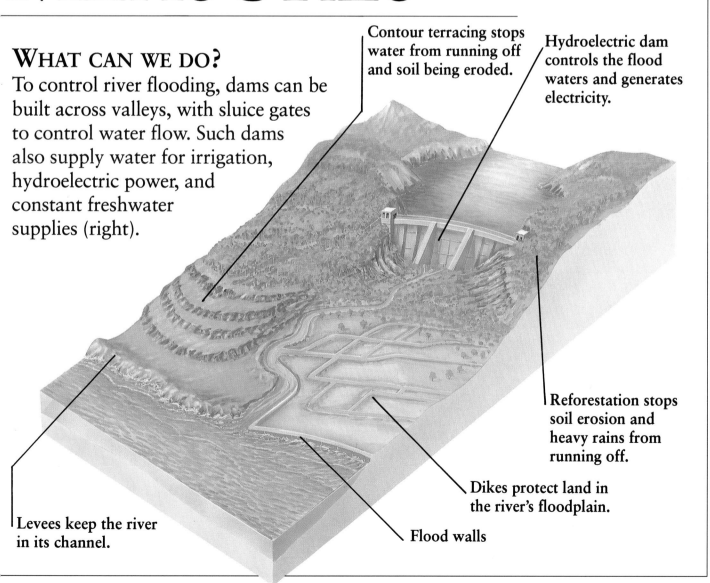

Contour terracing stops water from running off and soil being eroded.

Hydroelectric dam controls the flood waters and generates electricity.

Reforestation stops soil erosion and heavy rains from running off.

Dikes protect land in the river's floodplain.

Levees keep the river in its channel.

Flood walls

Myths about a great flood have been told all around the world. Ancient and devastating floods probably gave rise to these stories because it may have seemed to primitive people as if the whole world – or as much of the world as they knew – had flooded.

Hawaiian tales

According to the myths of Hawaii, the flood, Kaiakahinalii, destroyed everything alive, except for two people. Nuu built a great vessel and survived the flood with his wife, his three sons, and their wives. In time the flood waters receded and Nuu's vessel came to rest on Hawaii's highest mountain, Mauna Kea (above).

MYTHS AND

TWO TALES OF THE FLOOD

In The Bible, God decided to destroy humanity with a great flood. He only warned Noah and his family, who built an ark (right), and saved two of every kind of animal. To the Chippewa tribesmen of the Far North (below), the spring floods were caused by a mouse that gnawed a hole in a bag that held the sun's heat. This melted all the snow, causing a great flood.

In 1929, an unusually thick layer of clay was found near the Euphrates River in Iraq (right). It was caused by floodwater around 3200 B.C. This flood may have given rise to the Biblical flood of Noah.

LEGENDS

Greek stories

In Greek mythology, Zeus (below) sent a flood to destroy humanity. Warned by his father, Deucalion built an ark. He survived on the ark with his wife for nine days and nights. On the tenth day they grounded on Mount Parnassus. Zeus then granted Deucalion's wish to renew humanity.

Good farming
The Nile River was once one of the best known examples of putting floodwaters to good use. Its late summer floodwaters turned the land around the Nile into fertile land for farming (below) by depositing nourishing sediments.

easonal floodwaters may serious damage. But it's not all bad. Such predictable flooding has been put to good use by humanity for thousands of years. In ancient Egypt, for example, the people depended entirely on the Nile; without its water and its annual flooding Egypt would have been an empty desert, with no farming.

IT'S NOT

THE ASWAN DAM

The Nile River was expected to flood every year. Sometimes the flooding would be too severe, and people were taken by surprise. The Aswan Dam across the Nile has prevented two such floods (1964 and 1975) by holding back floodwaters, as well as two droughts (1972 and 1983) due to water supplies stored in the reservoir (Lake Nasser) behind it.

ON CLOSER INSPECTION
– *Terracing*

In places, such as Bali and the Philippines, hillsides have been cut into steplike terraces for thousands of years. These terraces capture the rain water during the monsoon season, providing constant irrigation for crops, such as rice, and also keeping the fertile mud in place.

ALL BAD

MAKING THE MOST OF IT

The floodplains of the Mekong River in Vietnam (below) and the Ganges River in India provide perfect land for the growing of crops, such as rice. The farmers of these places build walls around their paddy fields in order to keep them continually flooded during the growing season (left).

Florida

If global warming does occur, over a few hundred years sea levels may rise between 13-26 ft. Whole cities would disappear beneath the waves. In such an extreme situation, much of Florida (see below) would be flooded. St. Petersburg and Miami would be underneath the sea, just like the lost city of Atlantis.

Fort Walton Beach

Jacksonville

Tampa — St. Petersburg

— Miami

Present day

13-26 ft rise in sea level

RISING SEAS

Global warming has resulted in the average sea level around the world rising 0.5 inches per decade over the last century. If CO_2 emissions aren't reduced, global warming may become a serious problem. If nothing is done this rate may increase, causing the sea level to rise by 1-4 inches per decade.

Scientists studying "global warming" – the increase in world temperatures – believe that it could result in more tropical storms, tidal waves, and storm surges. Global warming is caused by an increase in the "greenhouse effect" – the effect that keeps the earth warm enough to support life. If global warming continues and weather patterns change, severe flooding may be one of the results.

WATER, WATER

ON CLOSER INSPECTION
– *Good points, bad points*

The Mississippi River may be feared as a source of major floods, but it has its uses – it is essential to the oil industry. It takes about 2,000 gallons of water to refine one barrel of crude oil. The Mississippi provides enough water for 340,000 barrels of oil to be produced every day.

EVERYWHERE

Greenhouse effect

CO_2 is one of the "greenhouse gases" that traps the sun's heat in the atmosphere, producing the greenhouse effect. Like glass in a greenhouse, they allow the sun's rays through to heat the earth, but trap some of the heat that radiates back.

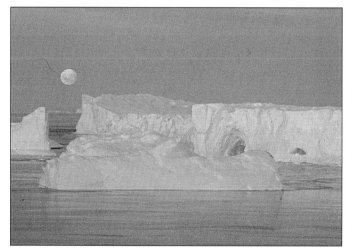

MELTING POLES

Scientists fear that rising temperatures may eventually lead to the melting of the great sheets of ice at the poles (above). The sea level would rise and drown low-lying areas, leaving places like the Maldives in the Indian Ocean (left) permanently underwater.

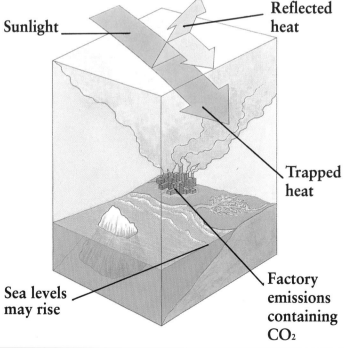

Sunlight

Reflected heat

Trapped heat

Factory emissions containing CO_2

Sea levels may rise

CHRONOLOGY OF TIDAL WAVES AND FLOODS

Location	Description	Year	Casualties
Lisbon, *Portugal*	Tidal wave	1755	60,000
Krakatau	Tidal wave	1883	36,000
China, *Yellow River*	Flood	1887	900,000
North America	Flood	1927	246
China, *Yangtze River*	Flood	1931	300,500

Severe flooding in the Philippines in 1991.

Location	Description	Year	Casualties
Nicaragua	Tidal wave	1992	170
Flores Island	Tidal wave	1992	1,000
Mississippi	Flood	1993	50
East Java	Tidal wave	1994	250
Sanriku, *Japan*	Tidal wave	1994	0
Jalisco, *Mexico*	Tidal wave	1995	1
Palu, *Indonesia*	Tidal wave	1996	24
Tuscany, *Italy*	Flood	1996	60
China	Flood	1996	2,000+
Spain	Flood	1996	0
Acapulco, *Mexico*	Flood	1997	400

The Yangtze River breaks its banks in China.

Location	Description	Year	Casualties
Florence, *Italy*	Flood	1966	35
Bangladesh	Flood	1970	500,000
Ishigaki, *Japan*	Tidal wave	1971	0
Northern Europe	Flood	1987	0
South Korea	Flood	1990	137
Bangladesh	Flood	1991	250,000
Shanghai, *China*	Flood	1991	1,300
Philippines	Flood	1991	2,000

Flooded farmland in the Sudan.

Atmosphere The mixture of gases that surrounds the earth. It provides some of the conditions needed for life.

Carbon dioxide (CO_2) One of the gases found naturally in the atmosphere. It is also produced by burning fossil fuels.

Condense When a gas cools and turns into a liquid.

Deforestation The removal of large numbers of trees from the landscape.

Dike A protective wall, usually built of earth reinforced with stone, which keeps water out.

Earthquake A violent, shaking movement in the earth's crust, which releases huge amounts of energy.

Evaporate When a liquid is heated and turns to vapor.

Fertile land Land that is suitable for growing crops.

Floodplain Land on either side of a river that is covered with water when the river bursts its banks.

Global warming An increase in the earth's temperature that may be caused by carbon dioxide and other greenhouse gases. It stops the earth's heat from escaping.

Gravity A force that pulls one object toward another. The earth's gravity pulls on all solids, liquids, and gases.

Greenhouse gas A gas in the atmosphere that traps the sun's heat and keeps the earth warm enough for life to exist.

Hurricane A spinning tropical storm that occurs over the Atlantic Ocean.

Levee A riverbank consisting of material dumped by rivers when they flood. Human-made levees keep the river water in its channel.

Mantle The layer of rock that lies between the outer crust and the core of the earth.

Sediment A mixture of rocks and soil that is carried along by a river.

GLOSSARY

Seismograph An instrument that measures movements in the earth's crust as wavy lines on a moving sheet of paper.

Silt A mudlike material made from tiny pieces of rock. Silt is a type of sediment.

Soil erosion The removal of soil by heavy rains and wind.

Storm surge A series of huge waves that are whipped up by a tropical storm.

Transpiration The process of plants giving off water vapor through their leaves.

Tsunami A series of huge sea waves caused by shock waves from an earthquake or volcano.

Typhoon A tropical storm that occurs in the Far East.

Water cycle The continuous movement of water from the oceans, up through the air to the clouds, and back down to Earth as either rain or snow.

INDEX

Photo credits

Abbreviations: t-top, m-middle, b-bottom, r-right, l-left.
1, 2-3, 5, 6t, 7, 8, 10, 11, 13, 14, 15tr & br, 16, 18t, 19 m & b, 20 l & r, 22, 23, 24b, 27t & bl & br, 28, 29t & m, 30: Frank Spooner Pictures. 6b: Roger Vlitos. 12: Science Photo Library. 18b: Rex. 19t, 25bl & br: Mary Evans Picture Library. 24t, 26 bl: James Davis Travel Photography. 21, 25t: Hulton Getty. 26br: Robert Harding.